Positive Sexuality

WORDS BY SARA PERRY   ART BY KYLIE A. SIVLEY

FOREWORD

As a nationally recognized sex educator with young children in my life, I've always found myself grasping at straws when looking for impactful material to discuss sexuality with them. Too many authors miss the mark on a pleasure positive and empowering framework... but not this one.

"Positive Sexuality," is the swiss-army-knife of sex education for young people and the supportive adults in their lives. Author, Sara Perry, does an incredible job of writing with intention on every page; using language that affirms and normalizes consent, bodily autonomy, pleasure, and ultimately liberation. Throughout the book you'll find beautifully drawn images proudly displaying a variety of internal/external anatomy, body sizes, and skin colors— something most children's book avoid with fear and shame.

Most of us have grown up in a world that shames sex and bodily pleasure, this book is a step toward undoing that harm. I encourage all readers to sit with the words, the imagery- the liberating message and reflect on what is coming up for you. Set intentions for the conversation or lesson with your young person that will follow this book. How can you use this to do better? To help create a world where sexuality is a freeing concept, not one that weighs us down with shame and stigma?

Sara Perry has done a large part of the work...and now it's up to you, to me, to us, to continue on in our fight for a pleasure positive world.

Stephanie Zapata
Educator & Speaker for Sexual Liberation

www.stephaniespeakshere.com

It doesn't matter how tiny or gigantic you are:

IF YOU ARE PINK OR CINNAMON,

if you have big hair or no hair,

if you have legs that run fast or no legs at all.

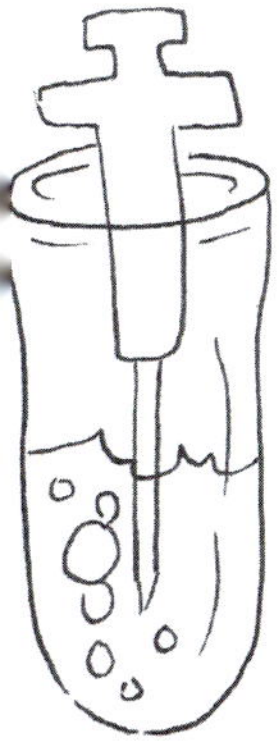

You are a person, perfectly put together.

7 feet (perfect)
6 feet (perfect)
5 feet (perfect)
4 feet (perfect)
3 feet (perfect)
2 feet (perfect)
1 foot (perfect)

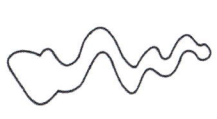

The way you look on the outside is made up of

what you are born with

+

WHAT YOU CHOOSE

Most people are either born with a vulva or a penis.

There are people who have both, too.

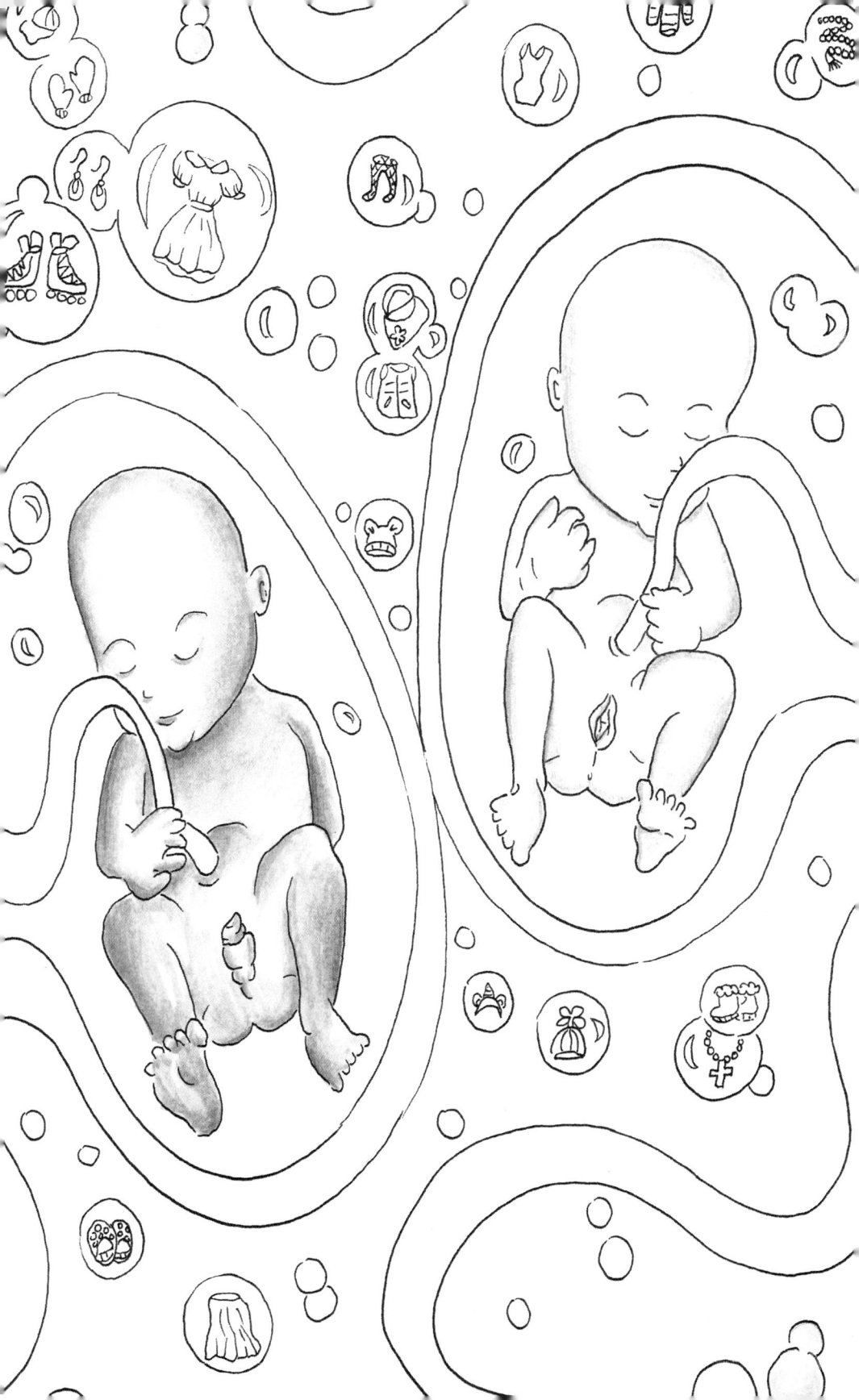

Having a vulva, a penis or both doesn't really mean anything other than those are your body parts.

YOU CAN CHOSE WHAT YOU LIKE AND WHAT YOU LIKE CAN CHANGE AS MANY TIMES AS YOU WANT!

You don't have to hold back tears or like playing with trucks or wear dresses or keep yourself tidy. You don't have to want to have a family, or a certain job, or explain to people any of the things you love.

We use words only to be able to talk to other people and to get them to understand what we mean, but ALL words are open to how you define them.
("boy", "girl", "tough", "whiny", "gay" can all mean different things to different people).

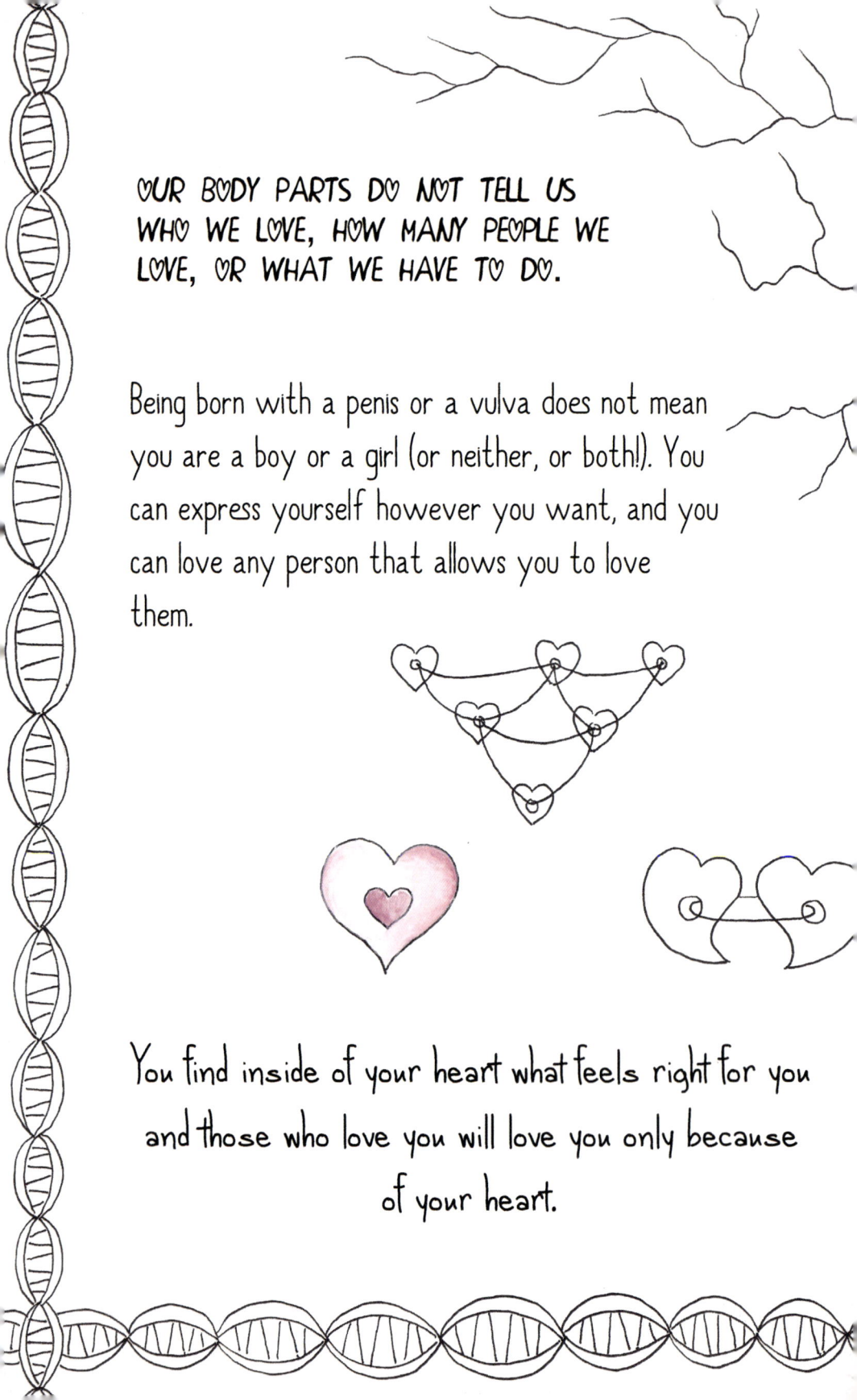

OUR BODY PARTS DO NOT TELL US WHO WE LOVE, HOW MANY PEOPLE WE LOVE, OR WHAT WE HAVE TO DO.

Being born with a penis or a vulva does not mean you are a boy or a girl (or neither, or both!). You can express yourself however you want, and you can love any person that allows you to love them.

You find inside of your heart what feels right for you and those who love you will love you only because of your heart.

We respect and support
EVERYONE in our human family.

People can choose to share their bodies with other people as a way to show love or feel good.

SOMETIMES SHARING YOUR BODY CAN MEAN HOLDING HANDS,
SOMETIMES IT MEANS KISSING ON THE MOUTH,
SOMETIMES IT MEANS TOUCHING ALL PARTS OF ANOTHER PERSON'S BODY

YOU GET TO CHOOSE WHAT SHARING YOUR BODY LOOKS LIKE FOR YOU.

Some people choose to love and share with just one person at a time, some people choose to love and share with many people at the same time and still others choose not to show their love through sharing their bodies.

Your body and your heart tell you when and if you want to share any part of your body with someone else, and you can always share as little or as much as you want.

We make sure we pay attention to the clues other people give us about what they like, too. If we can't figure out the clues, we just ASK.

Your voice is the is the only one that matters when you are choosing what to do with your body.

We trust people to decide what is right for them, too.

We don't convince someone to like us, and they respect us when we say no, too.

Our penises and vulvas are part of the areas in our bodies that have special power in them to make new people, and to feel amazing. We call these parts our reproductive organs.

To make new people (or reproduce) it takes two parts:

A special seed called sperm (with an attached tail to help it move)

And a perfect home for it to grow called an egg (it's also called an ovum)

Inside the vulva-having person's body, the sperm will race into the uterus and to the fallopian tubes, where the egg waits. Only one sperm makes it in.

NOTE: The one sperm and one egg can split to become two people, and sometimes, there are two eggs waiting. This is the two ways twins are made.

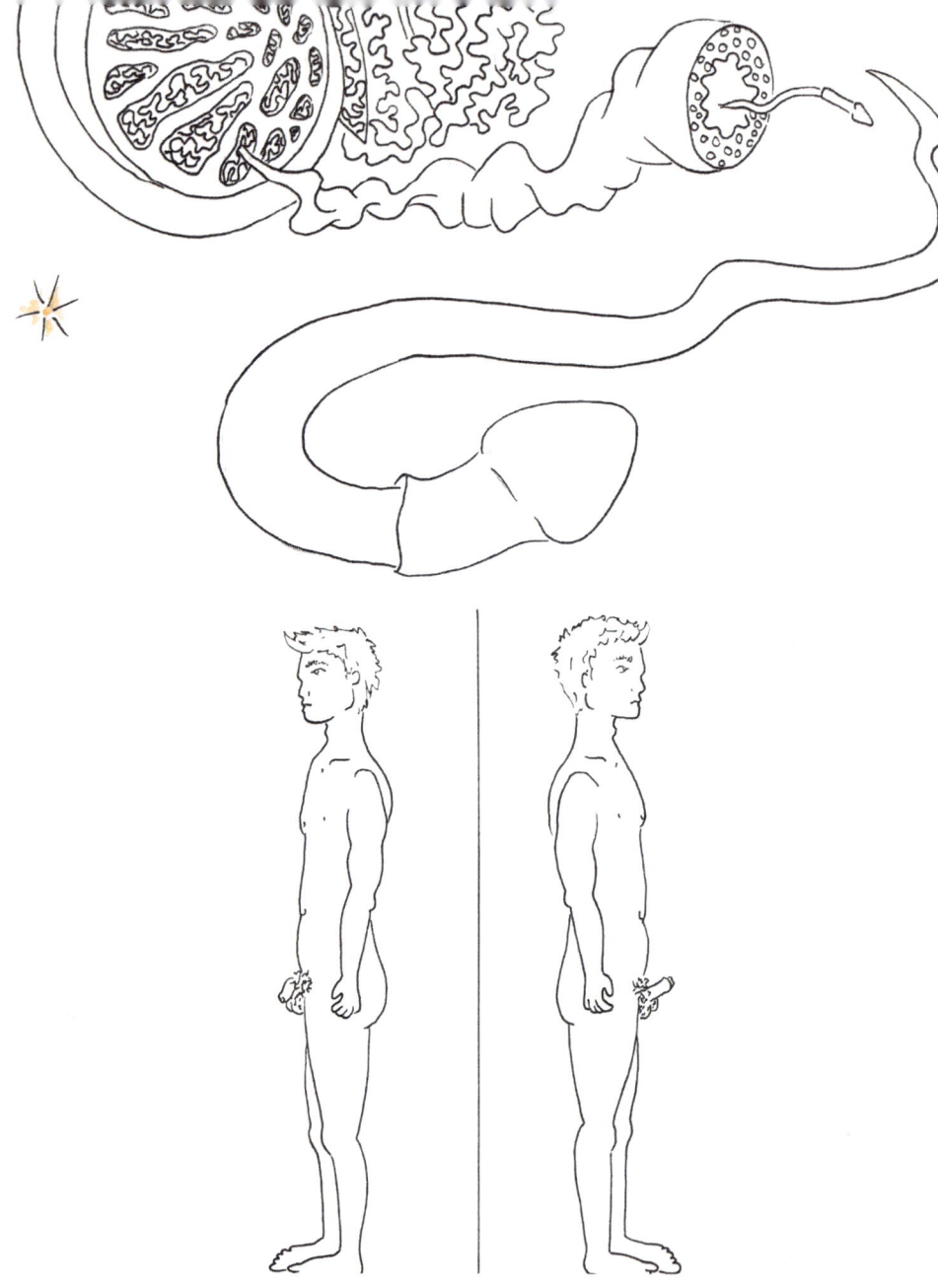

Penises are soft and bendy most of the time, but touch and thoughts can make them grown, stand up and get harder. This is called an erection.

ERECTIONS, LIKE PENISES, COME IN ALL SHAPES AND SIZES, AND THEY ALL FEEL AS GOOD AS EACH OTHER.

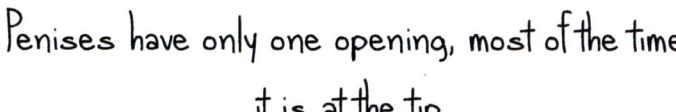

Penises have only one opening, most of the time it is at the tip.

Some have loose skin over the end and some have had it cut off as babies (this is called circumcision) so it is tight to the shape, and they look different than each other.

Penis-having people make sperm most of their lives in two hanging pouches under the penis called testicles (or testes).

They are VERY important and they have to stay safe, so they hurt very much when they are hit. They are also SMART and move to make sure sperm is protected. Because of this, testes shrink close to the body if they are cold or hurt, but drop further away if they are too hot.

NOTE: Males also urinate through the same opening that they release sperm from, but they are not the same thing and they do not happen at the same time.

People with vulvas have all of their reproductive parts inside of their body, so to take a look inside, we have to have pictures.

The part that we can see are the outer lips (labia) of their vulva. Below the outer labia there are inner labia, a bump covered in wrinkly skin called the clitoris and underneath, 2 openings.

The top one is the tiniest, but you probably can't see it, even with a mirror—this is where urine comes out. It is called a urethra.

The second opening is the vagina, and it can stretch big enough for a baby to come out of (and go right back to normal, after!).

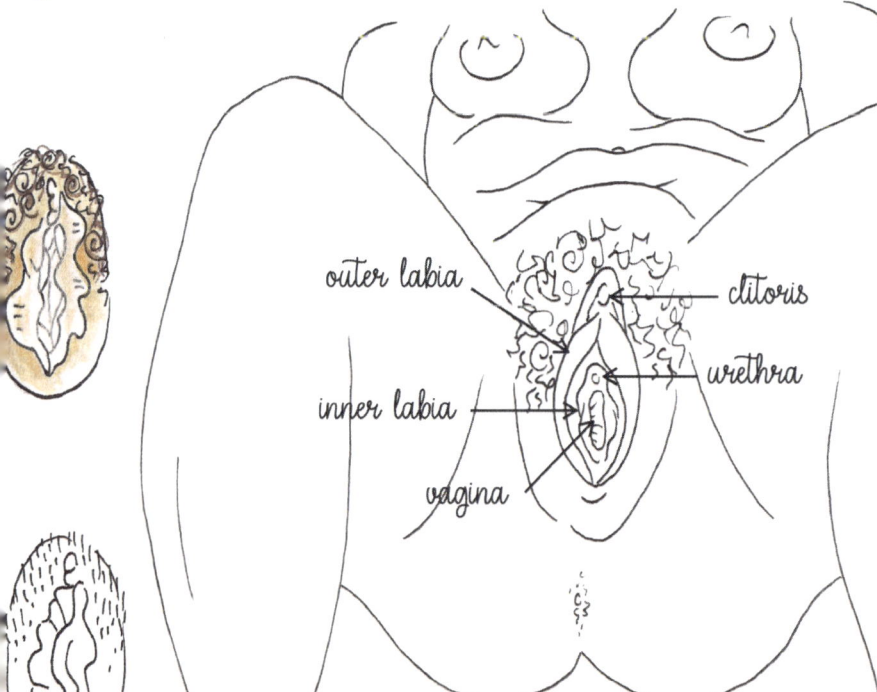

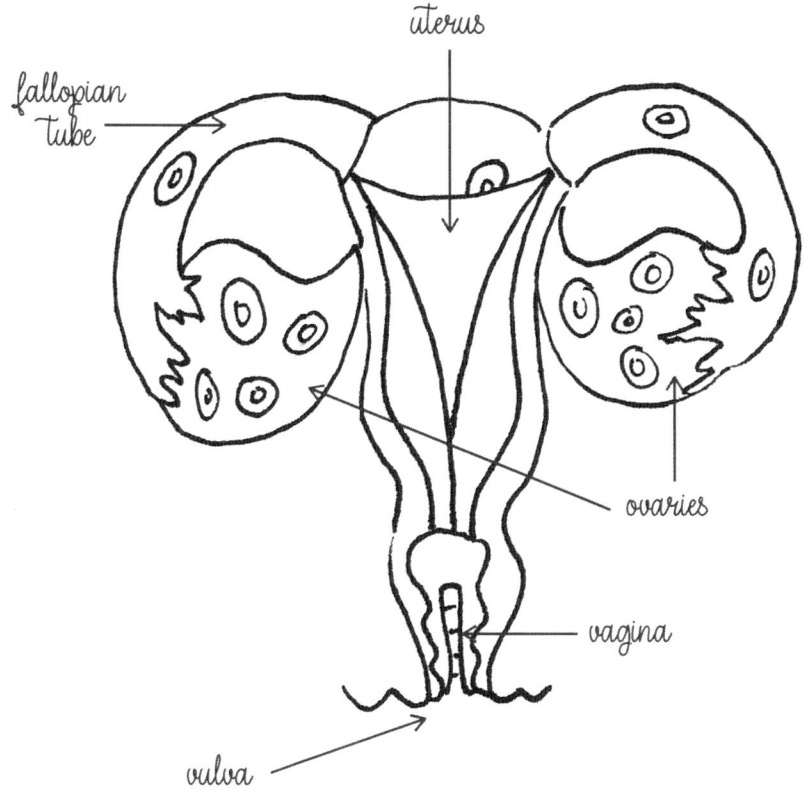

Inside the vagina, people with vulvas have a uterus where a baby can grow, and (fallopian) tubes that connect it to the ovaries.

The ovaries serve as the nests for the eggs they have. They are born with all of the eggs they will need in their lifetime.

Vulvas and labia come in all shapes and sizes.
They all feel wonderful.

People with vulvas together with people with penises can share their bodies to make babies, but most of the time people with any body part share their bodies because it feels good to them.

With the right touch and time, a vagina will become very slimy. When they are ready, the vulva-having person slides the penis or other body parts/tools into their vagina.

Then both people move their bodies in the direction and timing that feels best to both of them, like dancing to music.

Once a penis is ready, a liquid with millions of tiny sperm gets released (if they are sharing with a vulva-having person, it's usually deep inside the vagina, where it has the best chance at reaching the egg). This is called ejaculation. The penis then becomes soft again.

People call sharing bodies this way many things. Some you may have heard are: sex and making love.

Nature is SMART so our bodies have specific places that help us feel amazing when touching ourselves and when sharing our bodies.

In people with vulvas, the clitoris and places inside of the vagina (like a fleshy spot towards the top called the g-spot) can also feel wonderful.

A penis also has very sensitive skin all over it, but especially on the tip (where the sperm comes out), and it can feel great just to rub or pull it. It can also feel good to rub or pull the skin around the testicles (carefully!).

> IT'S VERY IMPORTANT TO LEARN WHAT FEELS GOOD TO YOU AND TO KNOW ABOUT HOW YOUR BODY WORKS! YOU ARE FREE TO MAKE YOURSELF FEEL AMAZING— THIS IS CALLED MASTURBATING. FOR NOW, IT IS BEST TO DO THIS ALONE AND IN PRIVATE..

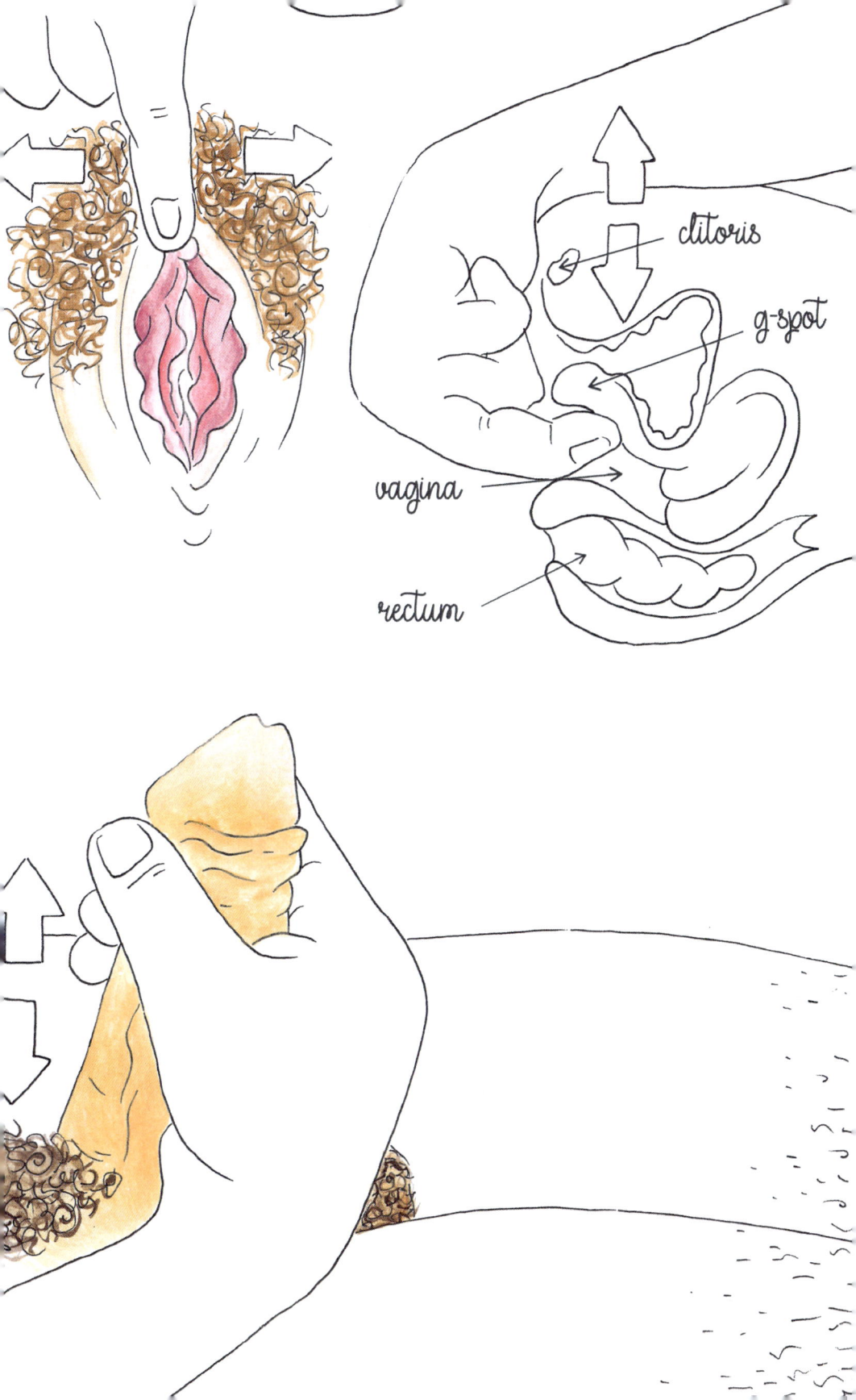

Touching these places that feel great for enough time leads to an explosion of feel good emotions called an

YOU CAN HAVE ORGASMS ALONE OR WHILE SHARING YOUR BODY.

Most of the time, the people sharing their bodies will take turns having orgasms because every body works at its own time.

NOTE: While people with vulvas can have orgasms at almost any age, people with penises cannot have them until they are ready to release sperm (typically around 10-13 years old).

All people can enjoy the touch of different parts of their bodies outside of their reproductive organs.

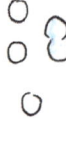

It's important to remember that our whole bodies were meant to feel great.

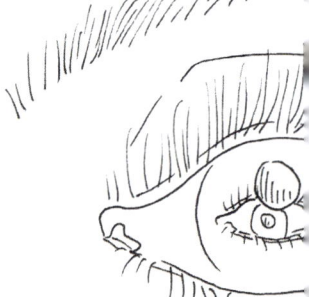

This means that every part of you- from your hair to your toes (even things you see, taste and smell!)- can be something that you enjoy touching and sharing.

SOME AREAS THAT PEOPLE ENJOY TOUCHING AND KISSING INCLUDE NECK, BACK, LIPS, NIPPLES, STOMACH, ANUS AND EVEN FEET.

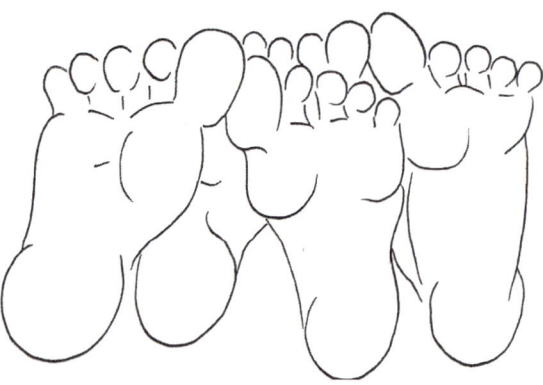

During a time called puberty, our bodies change from the bodies of young children, to the bodies of adults. Sometimes people think that it will happen slowly but everyone is different.

One day you will wake up and find coarse dark hair in your pubic area or underarms, swollen nipples or just that you smell strange.

YOUR FEELINGS TOWARDS OTHER PEOPLE AND YOURSELF MAY ALSO CHANGE.

All of these are normal and they are signs that your body is getting ready for the next stage of life.

When the body of a person with a vulva is developed enough to make babies, it starts to release eggs.

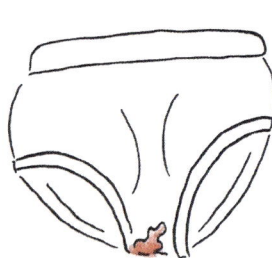

Every month, an egg will be released from an ovary, that is available to get fertilized and allow a baby to be made. If no baby is made, the cushiony sides of the uterus will wash out of the vagina to grow new cushiony walls..

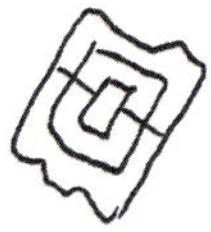

When it falls, it looks a bit like thick blood and it lasts about 3-5 days. We call this a period (it's also called a menses or menstruation).

People have many choices for how to stay clean during this time, (including pads, tampons and cups) and we are respectful and helpful in case they feel cramping or need extra support. We allow people to tell us how we can help if they want us to, and respect them if they do not.

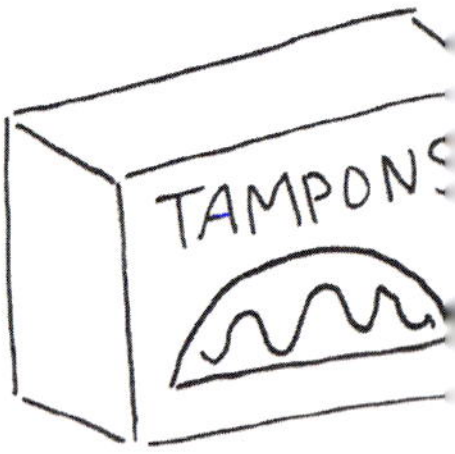

Some people have only tiny, thin amounts of liquid come out, others have a lot at a time. Sometimes you can feel it coming out but it does not hurt. Some people feel grouchy or sore, but not everyone.

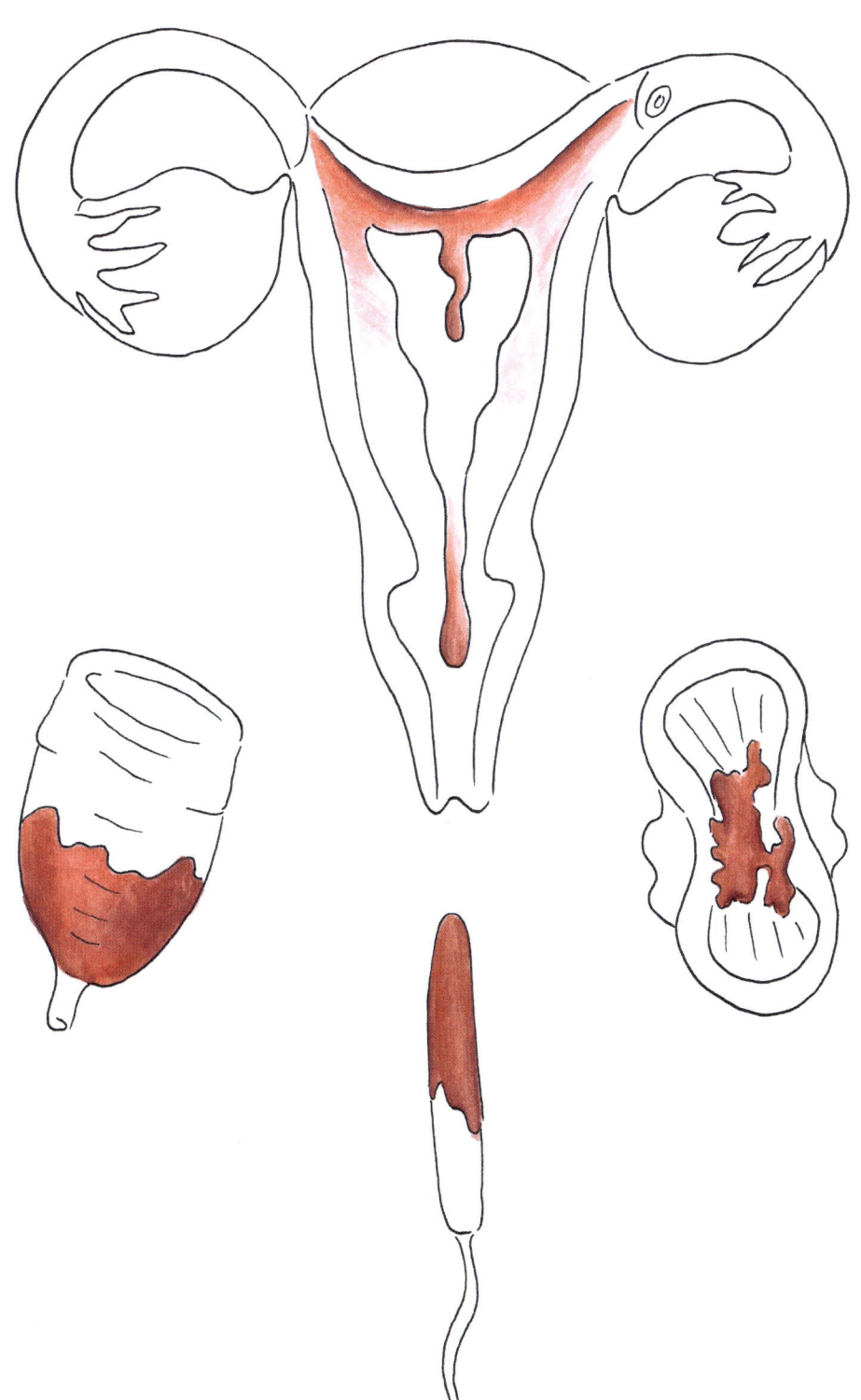

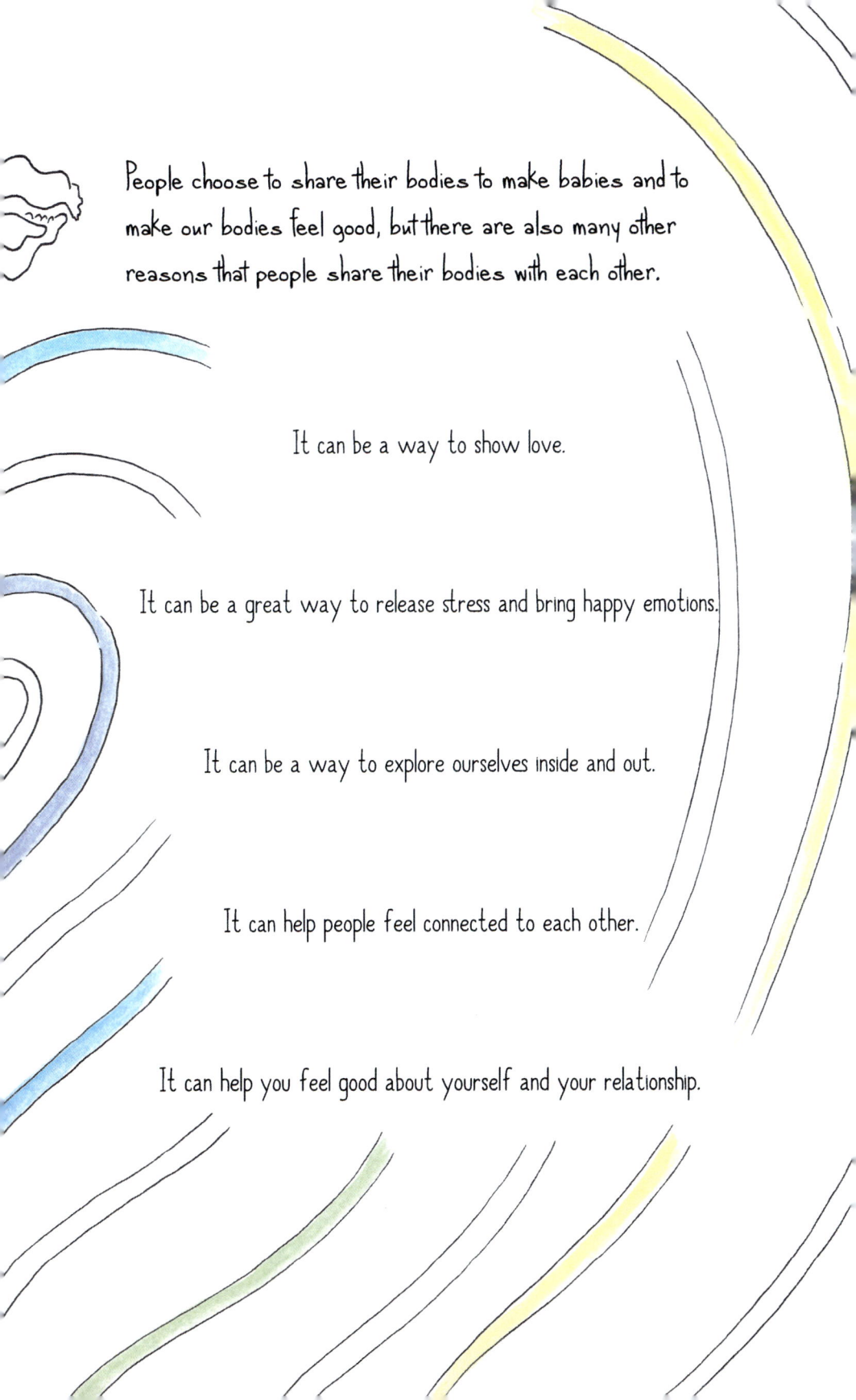

People choose to share their bodies to make babies and to make our bodies feel good, but there are also many other reasons that people share their bodies with each other.

It can be a way to show love.

It can be a great way to release stress and bring happy emotions.

It can be a way to explore ourselves inside and out.

It can help people feel connected to each other.

It can help you feel good about yourself and your relationship.

Sometimes people who you have not given permission to share your body can make efforts to make you share it.

If you do not want someone touching ANY part of you, you can say "no!" and that has to be respected.

A person who is not listening when you say "no" is not taking care of you.

If a person in your life is forcing you to share your body, telling a trusted adult (like mom, dad, teacher or doctor) will help make sure it stops happening.

ASK for Support!

Remember that you can say "no" ANY time, even if you said "yes" earlier. Staying quiet does not mean you said "YES".

IF SOMETHING IS HAPPENING THAT IS MAKING YOUR HEART FEEL UNCOMFORTABLE, TRUST YOUR HEART.

YOU ARE THE BOSS OF YOUR BODY.

When you are ready and if you choose to, sharing your body with another person can feel wonderful to your body AND to your heart.

We know we are ready when:

- [ ] We can talk to the person we want to share with and not feel embarrassed or uncomfortable.

- [ ] We feel safe with ourselves and with the other person

- [ ] Our heart feels happy when think of sharing and when we share our bodies with them

- [ ] We don't feel like we have to keep that happiness a secret

- [ ] You know what makes your body feel good and feel happy talking about it so the person you choose can know what you like, also.

- [ ] You feel confident saying aloud how much of your body you want to share (even if you change your mind in the middle of it)

- [ ] You can talk to a trusted adult (like mom or dad!) about how your body and your heart are feeling

- [ ] You trust that you will be understanding if your partner asks for something different

- [ ] Your body and your heart tell you they are ready

- [ ] You can be honest about who you are and what you like with you partner's (those we love deserve to know us!)

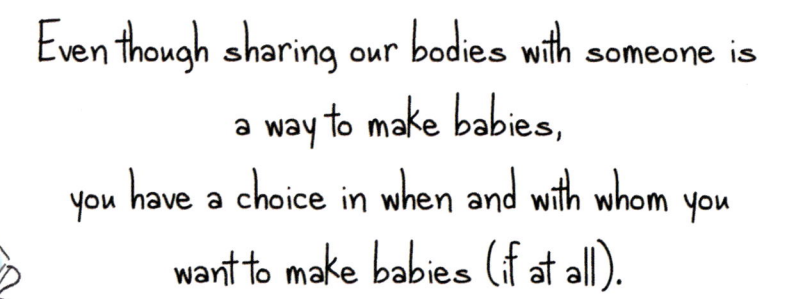

Even though sharing our bodies with someone is a way to make babies, you have a choice in when and with whom you want to make babies (if at all).

A vulva-having person's body is only able to make babies once their first egg has been released (typically around 10-16 years old).

Even after that, there are many choices for people who don't want kids.

One of the most common choices is called a condom. It is a rubbery glove that slides onto the penis and has extra room for sperm to be collected. It's also helpful in stopping certain diseases that can be spread through body sharing.

Some diseases that can spread through body sharing cannot be cured, but you can learn how to stay safe. There are also many ways in which people with these diseases can still share their bodies and feel pleasure.

Other choices include a daily pill that prevents an egg from being released, foams that contain a chemical that kills sperm, and simply choosing not to allow a penis to enter the vagina at all (this is sometimes called celibacy).

IMPLANT

PERIOD TRACKING

If you want more information about birth control, ask a trusted adult or your doctor.

DAILY PILLS

Remember that how to prevent pregnancy is your choice, and you are worthy of open conversations. You have the right to figure out what works for you.

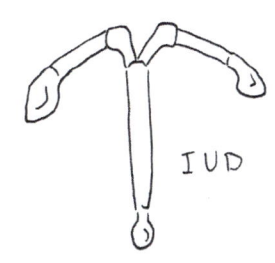

IUD

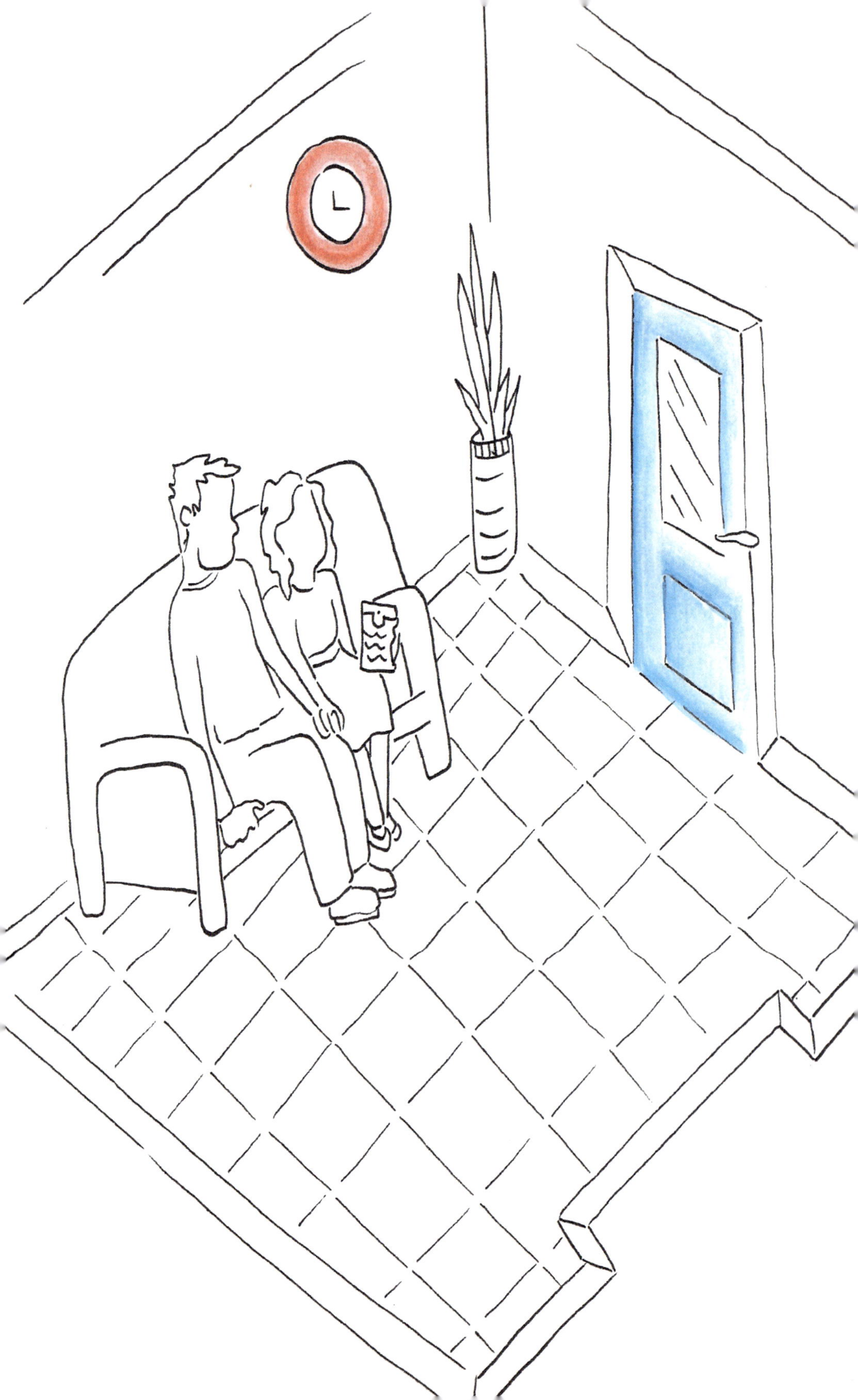

There are also choices for people if they are pregnant and do not want a baby.

No one's choices are the same as anyone else's. We are free to decide our joy and we are worthy of expressing ourselves.

We are valuable and worth loving exactly as we are, even if we make different choices than what another would have.

We support people having to make difficult decisions like these in their lives because everyone is doing what is best for them, and the world is a better place when we all can do the things that makes us happy.

i trust me with my body

The reproductive parts of your body are important, so just like your brain and your lungs, you need to keep them safe and protected.

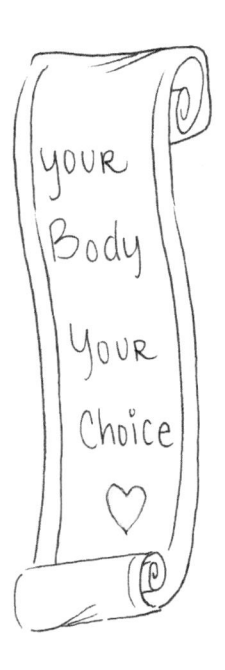

Your Body Your Choice ♡

Talking to your support system (family, friends) about your body, your pleasure and your happiness can help you figure out what fits your heart.

you've got This!

You are allowed to ask questions about how your body works and to decide when you want to share it with other people.

Learning how to love and enjoy our hearts and our bodies starts with learning to love and make ourselves feel wonderful.

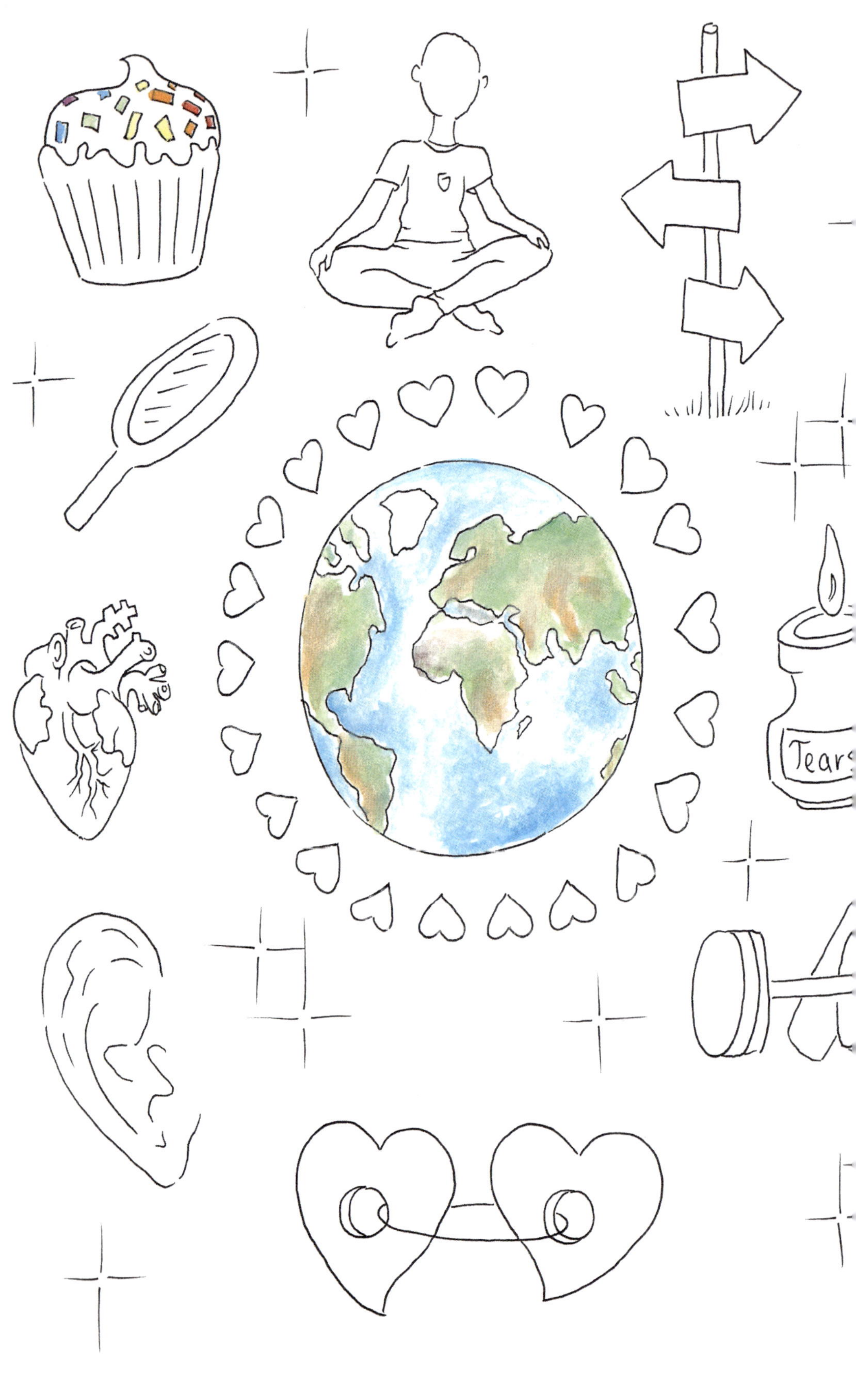
Tears

Words to live by:

I AM WORTHY OF RESPECT

I AM LOVED

I AM ENOUGH

I AM RESILIENT

I AM CAPABLE

I AM PROUD OF MY EFFORTS

I ACCEPT ANY EMOTION I FEEL

MY EMOTIONS DON'T CONTROL ME

I CAN CHANGE THE WORLD

I CAN WORK VERY HARD

I CAN RELAX WHENEVER I NEED TO

I DON'T HAVE TO EARN A CUPCAKE

EXERCISE FEELS AMAZING

I AM ALLOWED TO MAKE MISTAKES

I AM CURIOUS AND I ASK QUESTIONS

I APPRECIATE THE DIFFERENCES OF OTHERS

THIS EARTH IS WORTH TAKING CARE OF

MY HEART IS WORTH TAKING CARE OF

THE WORLD IS A BETTER PLACE BECAUSE I AM IN IT

I AM A GOOD FRIEND

I CAN LISTEN WITHOUT DOING ANYTHING ELSE AT ALL

I RESPECT EVERYONE IN MY HUMAN FAMILY

I SUPPORT EVERYONE'S CHOICES, EVEN IF THEY ARE NOT MINE

I LEARN BY MAKING MISTAKES AND ASKING QUESTIONS

I AM WORTHY OF SUPPORT

MY BODY IS MY OWN

I AM FREE TO DEFINE WHO AND WHAT I LOVE

I AM FREE TO BE HAPPY

Why are you still reading? the book is over...

Made in the USA
Columbia, SC
22 February 2021